BLOOMS

Francesca Cacciarru

ISBN 978-1-4710-8977-0

First paperback edition printed in 2012
Publisher: Lulu

For more copies of this book or general queries, please email:
ask4blooms@gmail.com

BLOOMS

PREFACE

The idea for this collection of poems came from my two-month journey across India, which began in June 2010. I wanted to write a story that would take the reader through the places I visited, the experiences, and all the reflections that came from them. While working on this book, I always bore in mind that the choice of poetry to convey this was in itself a challenge – prose being the most typical form of writing associated with stories. However, from the very beginning poetry seemed to be the only possible way: a sort of literary nootropic, until the end the most trustworthy – my memory's other half.

So here I break from a few structural differences between poetry and prose, wishing for each poem to carry a story, and story after story weave the tale of this extraordinary journey.

ACKNOWLEDGEMENTS

A number of people have helped make this book possible.

A special thanks goes to Sarah Law for her endless support and precious feedback, her patience and understanding, which were truly inspirational. Without her the book would not have been started or finished.

A most heartfelt thanks goes to Miroslaw Oleksy, my travel companion, whose passion and enthusiasm took me where I have been, both physically and spiritually.

I am also grateful for both the technical and emotional support of my brother Corrado, whose ideas and commitment were essential to the creation of this book.

A special acknowledgement goes to Zubin Patel and Sunny Singh, who helped me greatly with their cultural and linguistic knowledge.

I also thank my family and my long standing friends for their unconditional support and feedback – with a special thanks to Aleksandra Zur, who has always been the closest affection and the most avid reader of my work in progress.

Finally, I thank Derek and David Corbally, Rachel Brule, Parmod Sabharwal's family, Leena Patil Dwivedi, and the rest of the people I met along the way, whose friendships I treasure sincerely to this day.

Maps: Corrado Cacciarru; © 2009 ESRI, AND, TANA

Photographs: Miroslaw Oleksy

CONTENTS

47 days, 9 states, 7 capitals, 8.500 km, 7 wounds.

WE

He's in love with flying, this lovely guy -
a friend of mine who's bought
a ticket and shared his happiness online.

And now the shoot of a thought
has taken me and my sleep.
India! it shouts. I'd caught

it at my nape and now it's deep
inside my wakeful mind.
But I've already decided. It's *our* trip.

So this is one of the last times
that I am *I* and he is *he*, lying on
separate beds or bound to different paths. I'm

writing as the summer grazes London;
I'm leaving for the sand, the snow, the green
and all the things I've still no feel of

and you should know, as you go on, that *I* and *he*
most times will be just one. This voice will write as *we*.

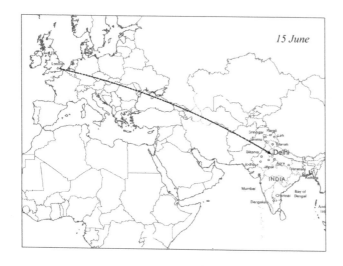

15 June

9

THE EYES OF THIS WOMAN TELL ME

The eyes of this woman tell me
off. And I'm just outside the airport doors.

Ladies and gentlemen...

The captain had announced
the landing and that dust
was just about as imminent.

...please remain seated with your seat belt fastened...

The eyes of this woman follow
me. They stare from a plump face that feels
so close to mine I can perceive

her body perspire.
It stands inside her dress, mellow
red to ginger out of shadow.

Welcome to Delhi...local time is 7.15...

The eyes of this woman give me
the same warning:
I should behave.

I should have been
attentive. I should have
listened to the captain.

*The temperature is 36.4...you should cover
your mouths with a scarf or a cloth,
and you should behave.*

*Yes, especially you, young lady, over there,
in Western clothes – travelling from
Europe – hey, cloth ears, think I didn't see
you didn't sleep a wink? You, foreigner, think
you can do whatever you want here?*

The eyes of this woman tell me
off. Come on, I thought, it's just a smoke!
So much for more than four

thousand miles away.
That's my father, but in a sari.

SOFTENER

Wrapping my towel around me
I smell London

The last wash
The one thing

That is untouched

Still.

The last wash
The one time

I smelt London
Wrapping my towel around me.

That is untouched

No more.

MUSTN'T BE HEAVIER THAN A THOUGHT

It was ridiculous
the way we laughed
around that roundabout!

All kinds of vehicles
outhorned each other in a mad
sort of harmony.

We waved like crazy people
to the slowest one, and watched it
approaching the sidewalk.

So the driver went
out of the jam and into reverse
to park it near us - just like a car -
between two cars.

He gave it a pat and
a sugar cane. But
when I stepped close to it I caught
what I'd never seen or even thought of.

So disarming

to stop the laughing.

The elephant's eyelashes.

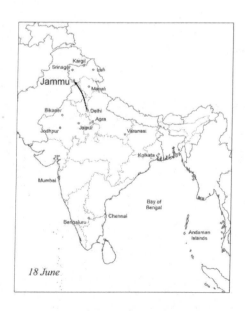

18 June

THESE TWO STRANGERS

These two strangers are
Amusing

Mango!
Elephant!

They really are.
Don't they know there is a war
A bunch of breaths
From here?

These two strangers are
Amusing

Cobra!
Coconut!

They really are
Worth having
In my house.
So please come

Honda!
Om!

This is my son – **a big boy of 16**
My dear daughter now will come – **she's 23** –
With a tray of fine *chai*

Do you have Facebook?
Shall we be friends?
Dad would like that too but he's no good
Let's stay in touch, all of us?

You make fantastic Dahl ma'am
She does, my wife, and rice and lamb and loves
You both already.

If you are not married
Are you brother and sister then?

No just friends but wait where are your plates?

```
We'll eat later
Now it's just you and dad and please
Have more, here, drink, try this
```

These two strangers are
Amusing

Would you sing?
Let's record them
Let's make sure
They will remember

THESE FOUR STRANGERS

CURFEW

With a handful of rupees
Among Kashmiri clothing
There landed
A dozen giant stones
On the unswept floor.

Hurry up please The young boy had said
All right what's up how much for this? We wouldn't care
That meanwhile
That outside
The day
Had turned for flashes

You've got to go I've got to close they're throwing stones
A start and
We jump on our *shikara*[1]
The young man's rowing
The old man's morning
Smile lies now flatter
Than the water

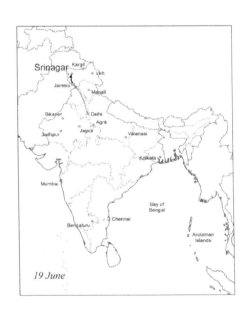

The dusk
Has seen Srinagar
In tear gas.

And then

    The night

It is the weirdest lullaby.

    It's calm

19 June

---

[1] A *Shikara* is a gondola-like wooden boat used on Dal lake for multiple purposes, such as transportation, fishing, and harvesting. It is a cultural symbol of Kashmir.

In its hatching calm.

    It lies quiet

It is obedient

    As a *bidi*[2] smoker

As the chanting[3] travels

    Placidly

Across the grey

    Dal Lake

It flows on,
    The city's lifeblood
And flows along
    Their inky blood
The shocking violence we hear of
    from a maharaja[4] to Lal Sharma[5] from a ragtag
    Pashtun army to the nuclear power to

    The *Jasmine Flower*[6]

    Floats

    On lazy ripples

---

[2] *Bidi* is a roll-up cigarette made of low-grade tobacco. It is popular among rural folk and the urban poor, in the South Asian region.
[3] The praying voices from the mosques were the only human sounds that broke the silence across the lake.
[4] Hari Singh, the ruler of Kashmir at the time India gains independence, in August 1947.
[5] Sham Lal Sharma, the current health minister in the National Conference-Congress coalition. He has demanded freedom for Kashmir as a solution to end the crisis in the troubled state.
[6] The name of the houseboat we stayed at, on Dal Lake.

On sleepy lotus

On brooding waters.

JULE

On the 21st of June I fell in love with *Jule*.

'Jule who?' you'd say, and do it little justice.
So try again, but read 'Joo-lay' this time. It's just
a little word and yet I fell in love – in *Little Tibet*.[7]

Please, let me introduce *Jule*.

First I caught it on the road to Leh,
where Nature had sprinkled
small handfuls of people
like stars on the mountains.

Hello!

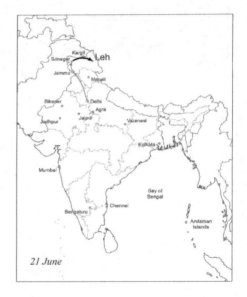

Then I caught it in the size of the sun;
the cheeks of this child
are burnt but won't hurt as they
puff out a smile.

Thank you!

I caught it everywhere
as I stared at the wind and
the Palace prayer flags danced
in slaps of colours on their cords.

A young monk walks along
the wheel as the air spins
his prayers. They elevate
in the orange sky, I wave *goodbye*.

Jule[8] *Little Tibet.*

---

[7] Ladakh. This region of Jammu & Kashmir is also called *Little Tibet* because deeply influenced by Tibetan culture. It is considered one of the last undisturbed Tantric Buddhist societies on earth.
[8] *Jule* is a Ladakhi all-purpose word that means 'hello', 'good morning / evening / afternoon / night', 'goodbye', 'please', and 'thank you'.

VIEW(S) ON HIMALAYA

Make sure you eat an egg
Hard-boiled is best of course
You know this air will make the most
Of your small lungs.

We stuff our backs with crackers and
Milk chocolate; I have a little headache
To neglect - for way too long.

Please rest. Oh God we're all alone, 5000 metres
High but hey, you know,
Another thousand and we'll sit
On the pillows of the sky.

Make sure you eat this egg
No thanks, can't even smell the sweet of milky tea
I'll eat what I have brought when I'm on top.

Please stop.

My mum makes a lentil soup no Dahl can top and yes she makes
My bed when I go there and I am sure stares
At my bed when I am far She definitely is
My favourite being in this whole world I shall make sure she knows
When I get home

Relax! Get in the tent and tomorrow we'll descend.

My friends,
I'm keen on dying.
I could take it gently I
Would embrace it morbidly
Until there is nothing I have to do
And nothing isn't complete
And nothing is yet to be accomplished

Ok that's it please talk, ok let's go, let's try to walk
Our way back down.

My love,
I see you wrapped in our blue blanket
I see the ignition button - broken -
In the cooker
The word cooker itself The membership cards in my holder
Your Oyster wallet, your watch on the table I see all
The little things lined up in the bathroom shelf The chest
Of drawers The umpteenth hole I tore and then

No more.

'So you saw God?' he laughs.

COULD IT BE

Feet out
The paneless window
Eyes half-closing on this
Worn out *Waterland*[9] and weightless
Head on this familiar lap

There: I feel something weird.

Is this Peace?
Could it be, for once, my total
Disregard
of Time
Could it be, for once, It has the lower
Hand and I - yes I -
Have Time?

26 June

The current on
Beas River's banks and rocks
Is this Peace.

Could it be, for once, not calm but
Fierce?
As in floods
As total
As in floods for
As long as it lasts

There: I raft along.

---

[9] Graham Swift's novel, 1983.

UP HIGH (Part I)

Looking down at myself dangling
I seem to hear a Nokia tune clear ring.
'Are you going to get it?'
(The pilot's hands were busy with the strings.)

'No, no,' he giggles right behind me.
(I knew he wouldn't, but still,
his 'don't worry' reassured me.

The patches of trees below were
half the size of my toes
and people like pinpoints - on a blanket knitted
with many hues of green)

Is this happening? (I thought,
and smiled) Has a phone just rung right
in the middle of the sky?

THE WAY UP HIGH (Part I)

Looking at the man ahead
on my same path
on the way up my heart broke.

For the man's back, I'm sure,
was just about to snap.
Yes I'm sure it was much

more painful than my guilt. Even
more painful than the strength
that thought of him will have
inside my head.

(And I thought
I could stop that
ache and go back but

I wanted to fly.)

THE WAY UP HIGH (Part II)

The rucksack on his shoulders dwarfed
the skinny size of him.

The mountain underneath
his sandals was not steep – was rather

perpendicular.
We reached the pick where

the man sat and the pilot spread
the big sack out onto the grass.

(And then, when I'm just about to jump,
I'll forget all of the man's pains and those

swollen veins
exploding in his arms)

UP HIGH (Part II)

Looking down at myself dangling
over Solang Nala Valley[10]
(I forgot all about the man.

The pilot strapped me to the sack - which
thus became my seat - and then

himself to me.
He grabbed the strings and yelled
NOW RUN RUN RUN!
And did I run! towards the cliff as I dared
the pressure of air and then I launched

into the wind.)
My God, I think,
I love my fabric wings!

---

[10] Solang Valley, at the top of the Kullu Valley - 14 km northwest of Manali - is known for its sporting activities such as paragliding, parachuting, and zorbing.

'There are some 60,000 beggars in New Delhi,
most earning 50-100 rupees a day,
not much less than the working poor...
Most say they have no skills...
The majority of them are children. [11]

BEGGAR

You are tiny
Beggar.

Do you dream?

Because I do.

Why is it not you in this white shirt?
In the mouth
Teeth are mint

Why is it not me under that sack?
It must be heavier than
My desk

Your neck
Must be stronger than all
My limbs' press

My head
Lighter than this Dilli's[12] dust
Your feet lift

Before me
– for I am behind you –
The road ahead's so bright

Or so I dream – because *I* dream –
Don't you?

Before us
The road ahead's in dust.

Beggar I am
Tiny.

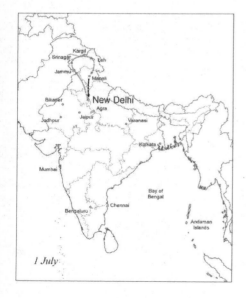

1 July

---

[11] *Inside the New Delhi Beggars' Jail*, by Sam Dolnick.
[12] *Dilli* is the local name for Delhi, India's capital and home to over 12.5 million people.

NAHARGARH

2 July

It was a miracle for breakfast,
as the poet wrote from a certain balcony.
It was still dark. One foot of the sun
served to remind me of something.

As a poet wrote from a certain balcony
at six o'clock, we were waiting for coffee,
served to remind me of something
– like kings of old, or like a miracle.

At six o'clock we were waiting for coffee
in the haunted fort[13] of the city painted pink[14]
– 'like kings of old, or like a miracle
revealing itself there and then' I thought.

In the haunted fort of the city painted pink
it was still dark – one foot of the sun
revealing itself, there. And then I thought:
it was *A Miracle for Breakfast*![15]

[13] Nahargarh Fort, built in 1734, overlooks the pink city of Jaipur, the capital of Rajasthan. A legend says that the Fort was named after prince Nahar, whose spirit used to haunt the place impeding its construction. As a result, a tantrik was called and the ghost agreed to leave the fort, on the condition that it would be named after him.

[14] In 1876 Maharaja Jai Singh II decided to have the entire old city painted pink to welcome the Prince of Wales. This colour was associated with hospitality.

[15] *A Miracle for Breakfast* is a poem by Elizabeth Bishop (1911-1979) written during the Great Depression.

IS IT SO, BIKANER?

It's just a game:
two camels and a cart
a bag of veggies and three pans, few songs
wheat flour, an unlocked phone, some
weary boxes of
water bottles
whose tops aim to the sky
in the sun some 49
degrees at ten.

It's just a game:
we've got two guides for these few days
they too play parts and right away
the one in white acts as the one
who must obey
the other man.

The other man
has got the reins,
he sings chews spits
smokes makes
chapatti[16] and all the choices.
He wears no trousers and is – in his checked *Dhoti*[17] –
the incarnation of masculinity.

We'd said goodbye once on our camel's back
leaving his courtyard
for this great Thar,[18]
his children running by the cart.

So then we start:
at night a silence game and then
a strangers' mimic play as soon as it gets bright
we ride for miles for

---

[16] *Chapatti* is an unleavened flatbread that accompanies many Indian dishes.

[17] A *Dhoti* is a rectangular piece of unstitched cloth, wrapped around the waist and the legs and knotted at the waist.

[18] The Thar, also known as the Great Indian Desert, covers an area of approximately 77,000 square miles (200,000 square km).

days of hills of sand
and swirls and shrouded ladies in the shade
of smiling dehydrated
mouths of
different tongues
Until we get
to the place we started from.

We've said goodbye once off his camel's back
back at his courtyard
for the last *ta ta,*[19]
all children
running, yelling, waving:
our dusty bus approaching.

It's just a game we'd said
feeding the fire and moon-gazing from our players'
sleeping bags.

But is it so, Bikaner?
Is it a game
to you
at all?

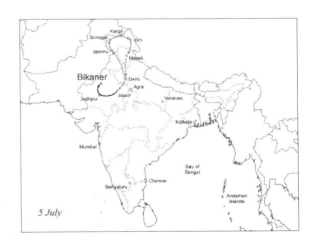

---

[19] 'Bye-bye'

THROUGH AGRA'S MAZE

O reassured soul!
Return to your Lord, well-pleased
and well-pleasing unto him!
Enter you, then, among My honored slaves,
And enter you My Paradise![20]

- The Holy Qur'an, Surah Al-Fajr: 89:27-30

And to think that the morning
smelt rancid, as we arrived,
slaloming through mountains

and mountains of rubbish.
Then the afternoon
got sleepy; only a cheeky

monkey lay in wait - way too close
to that fruit bowl.
Two chipmunks too, look out!

A little walk from cosiness we then received
A dozen smiles, and teas, and powders, creams
and chunks of ice on the face -

Beauty Saloon, it sort of read.
So that we'd be fresh when the sun falls
And when it did fall it was

A bright pink-orange on the terrace.
There, in the tickle of crickets,
another kite fight began.

A normal day,
through Agra's maze.

---

[20] The inscription on the southern façade of Taj Mahal Main Gate.

A NORMAL DAY

In 1648
The work of love

Completed Love itself.
Unearthly and yet

Of perfect symmetry
The ultimate

Refuge to soothed souls[21].
For over twenty years

He mourned.
Until the Sun

And then the Moon
Cried too

*A teardrop
on the cheek of eternity.[22]*

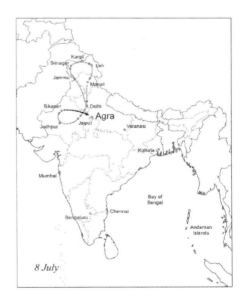

8 *July*

---

[21] The emperor Shah Jehan and his beloved wife Mumtaz Mahal, to whom he built the mausoleum.
[22] India's Nobel laureate Rabindranath Tagore described the Taj Mahal as such.

BY THE GANGES AND GANGA

The golden flames
Water the eyes

That linger on white sheets.
It is the sizzle that precedes

A wet kiss.
From Vishnu's feet

I have emerged.
Pretty and raised

In heaven
I would dance

In whim and laugh
I would be safe

In Brahma's love
Until a curse.

I'll leave for earth
And I'll be caught

Amid the locks
Of Shiva's hair.

The tentacles of fire
Flap and flinch on

Skin *and sins* until
They're ash.

I will see those   *I will swallow*
Chips of bones   *Chips of bones*

That once were whole
And holy at my touch.

                               I will be
                               Released in streams

                               To free the souls
                               Of Sagar's sons.

As the rain falls
A peaceful grey

Replaces the day above
The pyre. Pilgrims line

Along the river with
The hope they're given

Moksha.[23] I watch life,
And death,

At the burning ghat
Of Manikarnika.

---

[23] *Moksha* literally means 'release' and is the liberation from *samsara*, the cycle of death and rebirth.

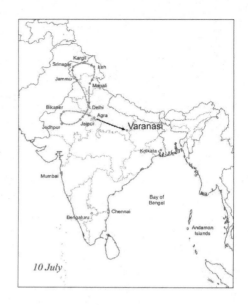

10 July

ANANDAVANA

I don't need to lie down to die
I'm writing from Hell or nearby

I stand among the dead
The clock has ticked again
this time the hour numbers five

Come on it's just a train that's just a little late let's wait let's sit

I stand
in dread and dirt bugs rats and flies
Can't leave this time, can I?
Can't switch to programmes on demand
Can't change my mind can't like and then unlike
as if online this is the hour number eight

*Come on stay put let's chat don't look around too much perhaps let's move
a little further you know how much we'll laugh when this is over*

But will it end? This is the hour number ten and
look at this
thousand people all around:
a carpet of shreds that rest entwined and yet
unmatched
to the rest
to the opposite universe

I may as well
lie down and die.

Come on lie down I know this isn't
What they say

They say this is the earth's most sacred land
the Ghats the bones the wood the gods
the dawn on boats the logs
in fire at dusk
but *Anandavana*[24] must
be but Hell or nearby.

'the forest of joy' that's what it means I checked the clock it's been
twelve hours that we're stuck

in the *forest*'s train station.
I can't believe I'd had tomorrow planned
for there's no use now
the blackest side of *joy*'s unveiled
tonight
in Hell or nearby

I've just lain down to die.

Wake up, look up, the train.

---

[24] *Anandavana* is one of the ancient names for the city of Varanasi, in the state of Uttar Pradesh. It directly translates as 'forest of joy/bliss'.

BLOOMS

Against the outside garden gate
a man had started with a paper.

He placed a second, bound a third,
a bunch of magazines and then
another batch from the last box.

Against the tree beside the news,
a man had started with a mirror

and some towels, a few combs
along new blades and scented
foam and he began
to spray a little water on
the stubble of a customer.

Beside the tree, across the news,
a man had started with a pan.

He rolled some dough, then turned
the flames on and a morning whistle too
to play along the clattering
of cutlery.

Beside the news, across the tree, before my eyes
Kolkata blooms.

The street corner has a barber's
a newsagent's
and a bakery
now open.

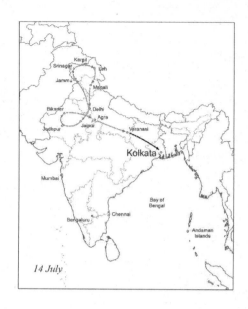

14 July

34

FACE UP

Face up
On the edge of an empty pool
There I lie
The blackest cloud outdoes
This clove of a moon
And She shows
And hides again
Playing

As if I feel like it.

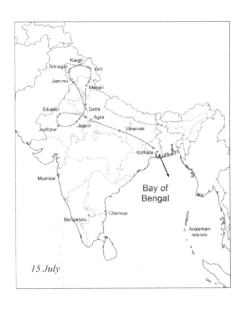

Face up
Cold concrete against the spine
There I lie I dive
In thought
I summon up
Those skilful jugglers of my mind
The armoured conjurers
Of night
And can't believe
I am, in fact,
Still.

Once up
On the edge of a brimming pool
Moments
To jump
Never could I have guessed
Pools weren't only for swimming.

WESTERN NONSENSE

I never know whether I want
to hug them or to punch them she declared and

How I loath them
for being such backward beings.

She had grown thinner and susceptible. She could swear these were
the most implausible of men.

That is what they are
Haven't they heard there are things like 'Don't stare'

'Don't touch' 'Don't spit'
'Queue up

for your turn'? No.
Shamans? Huh! she snorted.

They have heard none of
this Western Nonsense.

EASTERN NONSENSE

I never know whether I want
to hug them or to punch them she declared and

How I love them
for being so skilled, so bluntly unrefined.

She had got tanned and quite an appetite
for wonder. She could swear this was the way they truly were:

Shrewd and wise and sagaciously
shy as men. Huh! she said

This is primitive curiosity!
This is sheer deep kindred empathy!

But all balances destabilised,
all dichotomies reconciled,

Kya pata usay
Is sab k bare may.

36

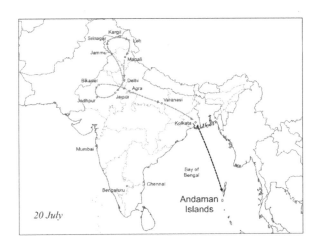

20 July

OVERNIGHT

NAMADNA, *says a pool of water, diaphanous on the morning after.*

The ship had anchored after five days of ocean's ire, and now it was the rain's turn. It fell sharp in silver needles. It felt cold, yet warmer than the puddles on the pier. Trying to make out what was around was difficult, but a glance ahead revealed a languid swish of grey palms bending in the dark. This felt so wrong! Ominous like an injustice, or more like a mistake: you don't get gloomy heavens, just like you don't get *Infernos* painted green. We bent our backs and got into the rickshaw. From its sides, as it moved, the wind felt icy on my wet clothes. The wiper went fast on the small windshield, but beyond its creak everything was constantly out of focus. Finally the driver slowed down before a wooden sign that read *Emerald Gecko*. Whatever that was, we went inside, got lock and key, then went to sleep in silence and soaking sadness.

There is no WELCOME *on its reflection – only* ANDAMAN & NICOBAR ISLANDS, *where*

> Bliss and its tinges
> surrender as under a
> tyrant: the Monsoon.

When I opened my eyes it was dark, but the roof of thatch sounded undisturbed.
I got up slowly – no rush to splash into the gloom – and realised that a frown
had imposed its print on my face like a fossil. And then I opened the door.
I stepped out of the hut and stood, staring. It was the colour that outside had,
and I was in it, and I remained in it, as still as air.

First a dive in white;
then sand meets sea and sky in
pale blue and turquoise.

It seemed as if an oneiromancer had been painting overnight. The Monsoon was
dormant, time lethargic, and around my warming feet there were

dry coconuts and
bamboo rafts – drifted ashore
from the near Myanmar.

TO HAVE FREEDOM THERE

Only one clean and dry T-shirt to wear
It's plain red and says FREEDOM in black
I bought it in Poland and wore it
in England, in Italy, in France
on planes and buses and cars.
This morning I put it on
inside out because I think
it'd be too much.

It'd be too much
on a bicycle.

On a bicycle
fast and barefoot on hot pedals – the glee
of swaying green eating up the road
to the *Elephant Beach* – I'll stretch
my arms out – the veils of scarecrows
dancing in the fields, swift as the kids'
pick beneath sapota trees – I stretch my arms out
to hug the air and the windy heat
fulfils my lungs. No locks
nor chains for bikes as we arrive
On the shore ours are
the first and only footprints.

Only one clean and dry T-shirt to wear
This morning I put it on
inside out because I thought
it'd be too much

to have FREEDOM there.

DOGS

As he hesitates
Hands on brakes
I kind of see it coming.

Dogs that bark don't bite
They say many miles away
But barking's just about
Enough.

I eye the dog:
It has grown small
Its soundless jerks quite laughable.
I can turn then
I can sigh then
The sage was right. Yes.
Though said nothing about ditches.

So when I think
That the worst's passed
That the dog's past
In fact
The present's twice as fast:

We crash.

SPIRIT

– A colourless, volatile, flammable liquid;

From Latin **spirare** *– To breathe, to blow, to play on the flute;*

spiritus *– Breath;*
Ghost;
Soul;

A boy (the doctor)
Whose age I first ignore
Eyes us softly and smiles
So pale a smile
That I guess just
How sorry he is

For us.

The doctor (a boy)
Whose age I quite ignore
Accompanies the door
That rolls its rusty course
On jagged hinges.

His hand on the room's handle,
His meek wrist nags it locked.
The wall has a sleek Krishna grin on –
A different pose for every month.
His flute reposes on a shoulder,
His blue legs crossed above July.

My eyes go round
And then I see it.
Among others, on the table,
Its label says

SPIRIT.

The boy's (God is only a boy)
Breath
Says sorry

He doesn't speak our language
But smiles
A pale apology

For us.

He takes the bottle
From the table
He pours the liquid
On our wounds.

The doctor – a boy a beast a ghost – a blur.

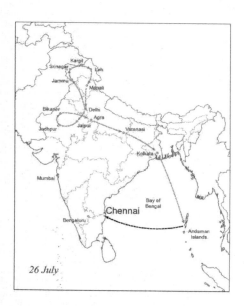

*T*he last time I
*H*ad a look at it on the
*E*arth I thought: it may

*S*eem that it only sits there -
*H*alf alone in the ocean,
*A*nd half attached to the rest -
*P*erhaps it does. In fact, it's rather
*E*vident. So what

*O*n earth have got inside my
*F*unny mind?

I neither know how
*N*or why it happened, but that
*D*ay I looked at the map and what
I saw was
A heart.

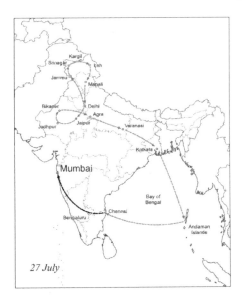

27 July

THE QUEEN

A master of shopping - her father's a scientist -
She grew in a big house, in the green outskirts
Of a dream. The Dream she now lives in.

She has a maid's mornings and graces
The two of us with great care.
Last night she washed my hair
And soaked his clothes, so
Now we're good to go.

Along the way she shakes off touts
Like crumbs on cloths, and calls a cab
Like it's a dog.

To the Queen's Necklace![25] she bawls -
And there we sit, where the bay at night
Makes pearls out of the lights.

Vada pav[26]? *Green chilli ice cream?*
This is Mumbai!
You don't go to what you want; anything you fancy
Comes to you (Bollywood too)

You see? Even the sink, she smirks,
Rinsing her fingers as the boy
Holds the bowl.

And now we smoke. Hey!
Hookah! Which flavour? I want apple.
And apple be it.
Is this apple? No wait,
Take it back,
I want mint!
So apple's changed

---

[25] *The Queen's Necklace* is Marine Drive: a C-shaped road along the coast of Mumbai bay. At night, the street lights resemble a string of pearls, forming a necklace.
[26] *Vada Pav* is one of the most popular and loved street food in Mumbai.

Just like everything else has

And what a change
In pace, for the last place
To bind our hearts with.

India? This is India?
She'd said, picture after picture, leaving
The last soft bite of her doughnut
Pending.

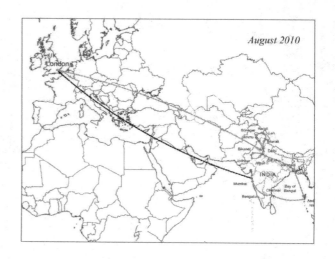

August 2010

THE BROKEN FLASK

So I'm back
To kettles on, to water bills
Lining the dishes in the dish rack.

I felt I'd lost my bargaining skills
Some time before I landed home
I lost them slowly, like magic swill

Drop by drop all spilled, all gone
I, the broken flask
Lost the winking eye, the meekest tone. Just one

Big smile I'll wear to mask
This mouth that shouts I'm sad.
So when they ask

'You're back, you're glad?'
I'll give the brightest 'yes'. Black-clad.